MW00667844

CHEF NANCY'S

Kids'

club

COOKBOOK

ISBN 978-193549708-0
Printed in Canada
Manufactured by Friesens Corporation
Manufactured in Altona, MB, Canada in October 2009
Job # 50421

Book design by Scott Stortz

Published by:

Butler Books
P.O. Box 7311
Louisville, KY 40207
(502) 897-9393
Fax (502) 897-9797
www.butlerbooks.com

Dedicated to my mother,

Adelaide Phelps Russman.

She not only taught me how to cook,

she taught me how to laugh.

CHEF NANCY'S

Kids' club

CONTENTS

Snacks

Wraps and Sandwiches

Sweets and Drinks

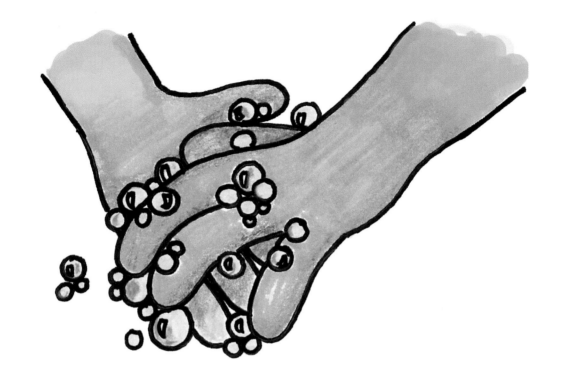

wasH youR HaNds
bEfoRE you cooK aNd
wasH youR HaNds
bEfoRE you Eat

SNacks

Ants on a Log

Bagel Faces

Graham Cracker Yummies

Kicked-Up Salsa

Brain Food

ants on a log

Be sure to wash all vegetables and fruit before eating.

INGREDIENTS

Celery ribs
Peanut butter
Raisins

1. Cut or break celery ribs into about 4-inch lengths

2. Spread peanut butter in celery

3. Put "ants", (raisins), on top of the peanut butter

bagEl facEs

INGREDIENTS

Bagel half   Mandarin oranges
Peanut butter Pineapple chunks
Raisins

1. Spread peanut butter on bagel

You can use cream cheese or soy butter instead of peanut butter.

2. Make a face using the other ingredients

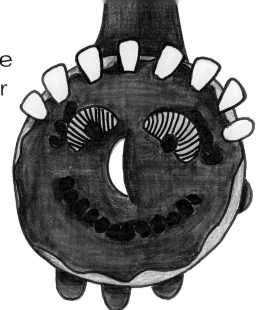

3. Take a BIG BITE!

GRaHam cRackER YuMMiES

INGREDIENTS

Low-fat cinnamon or
Honey graham crackers
Peanut butter
Mandarin oranges (small can, drained)
Ground cinnamon

1. Spread peanut butter
on the graham cracker

12

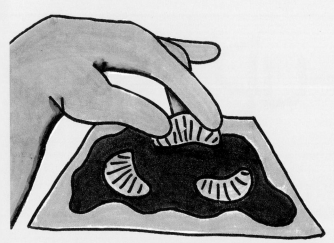

3. Sprinkle a little
cinnamon on top

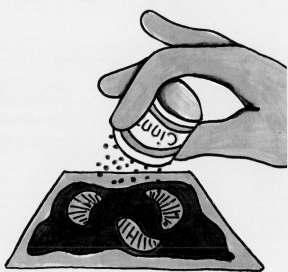

2. Put some Mandarin
oranges on top

KicKEd-up Salsa

INGREDIENTS

1 medium jar of
  your favorite salsa
1 can of black beans
Sliced jalapenos from the jar
Mozzarella cheese

1. Pour jar of salsa
in a big bowl

2. Rinse the
black beans
really well

14

3. Empty beans into the bowl

4. Add more jalapenos if you want

5. Add Mozzarella cheese to bowl with beans and salsa

6. Mix all the ingredients in the bowl

7. Eat with chips

bRaiN food

INGREDIENTS

1 regular size (16-ounce) box of vitamin-packed cereal
1 bag of vanilla yogurt raisins
1 bag of sweetened dried cranberries
1 can of low salt peanuts, low salt cashews, or low salt soy nuts
1 bag of mini-chocolate chips

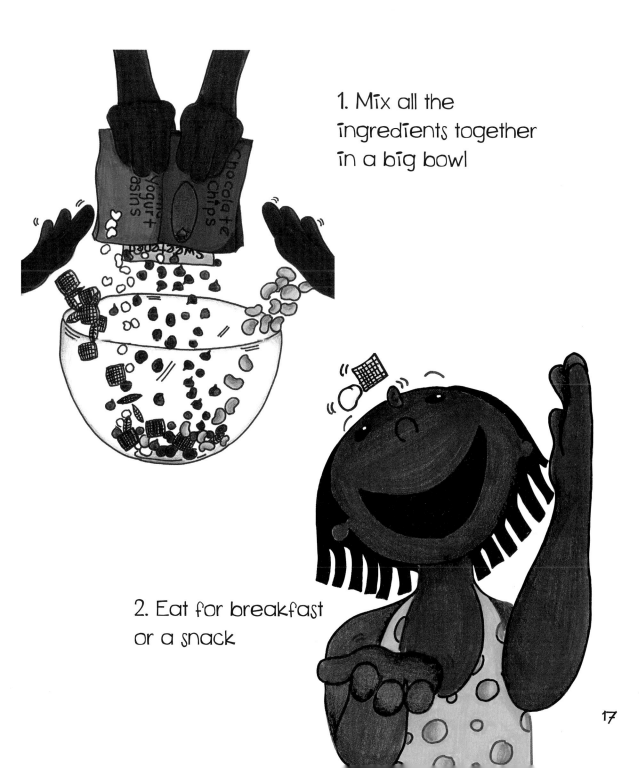

1. Mix all the ingredients together in a big bowl

2. Eat for breakfast or a snack

17

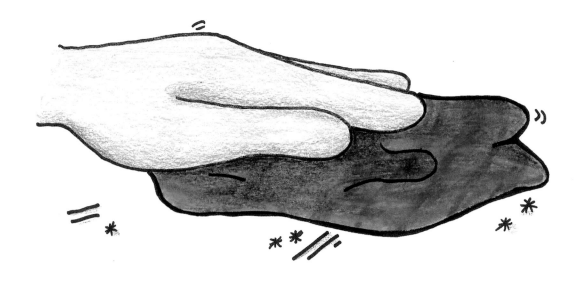

KEEp youR food SuRFacE clEaN

WRaps aNd SaNdwicHEs

Messy Apple Wrap

Rolled-Up Sunshine

Inside-Out Wraps

Slaw Dogs

Worms and Ants in the Grass

MESSy aPPlE wRap

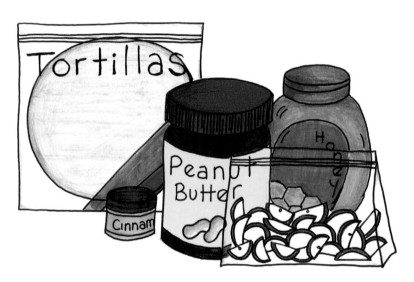

INGREDIENTS

Flour tortilla
Peanut butter
Apple slices
Cinnamon
Honey

1. Spread peanut butter on flour tortilla

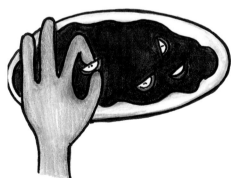

2. Lay apple slices on part of the tortilla

3. Sprinkle with cinnamon

4. Squeeze some honey

5. Roll up the tortilla

6. Eat with a napkin!

21

RollEd-up SuNShiNE

INGREDIENTS

1 flour tortilla
Cream cheese
Carrot (cut up or shredded)
Pineapple pieces

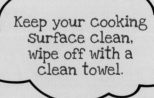

Keep your cooking surface clean, wipe off with a clean towel.

1. Spread cream cheese over tortilla

2. Add carrots on top
of cream cheese

3. Add pineapple
pieces to carrots

4. Roll up tortilla
and eat for lunch!

23

iNSidE-out wRaps

INGREDIENTS
1 piece of leaf lettuce
Sliced turkey
Low-fat Ranch Dressing

2. Put turkey on the lettuce leaf.

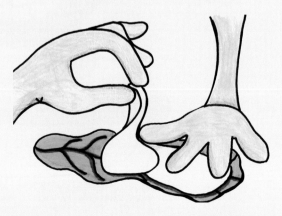

1. Lay lettuce leaf flat

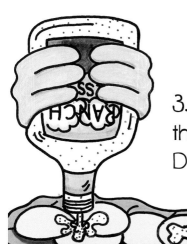

3. Squeeze some of the low-fat Ranch Dressing on the turkey

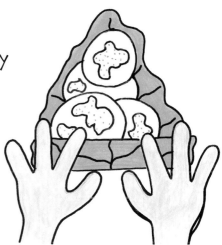

4. Roll up the lettuce leaf

5. Take a bite and laugh at your silly sandwich!

Slaw dogs

INGREDIENTS

1/3 cup of apple
    cider vinegar
1/3 cup of oil
1/3 cup of sugar
1 bag of slaw mix
Turkey slices
Hot dog buns

2. Put the oil, vinegar and sugar into a bowl

1. Measure out the apple cider vinegar and oil

3. Mix together
until the sugar melts

4. Add the slaw mix to the bowl
and stir really well

6. Put some of
the slaw on top
of the turkey in
the bun

5. Put some
turkey in a
hot dog bun

7. Open really wide and take a bite

27

WoRMs and aNts iN tHE GRass

You can also add matchstick carrots (orange worms) to go along with the string cheese.

INGREDIENTS
1 piece of leaf lettuce
1 piece of string cheese
Raisins

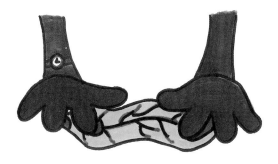

1. Lay lettuce leaf out flat

2. Tear string cheese into many strips (worms) and put on lettuce leaf

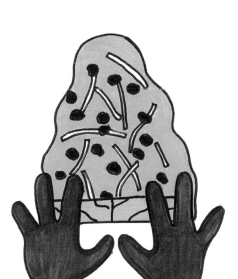

3. Sprinkle raisins (ants) onto lettuce leaf (see picture)

4. Roll up lettuce and take a bite!

waSH youR fRuitS aNd vEGEtablES bEfoRE you Eat tHEm

SWEETS AND DRINKS

Berry Cold O.J.

Creamsicle Float

Grapie Lemon Drink

Aunt Libba's Fancy Sherbet

Naughty Bars

Chocolate and Vanilla Swirl

Time Out Parfait

bERRy cold o.j.

INGREDIENTS

Your favorite frozen berries
Orange juice

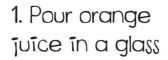

1. Pour orange juice in a glass

2. Put frozen berries into the orange juice

3. Sip the drink and eat the berries!

33

cREamSiclE float

INGREDIENTS
1 big scoop of low-fat vanilla ice cream
8 ounces of orange juice

1. Make a big scoop of
ice cream

2. Put the scoop of ice cream in a tall glass

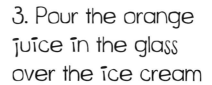

3. Pour the orange juice in the glass over the ice cream

4. Drink your float … you may need a spoon too!

GRapiE lEMoN dRiNK

INGREDIENTS

Lemonade
Grape juice
(or frozen grape juice)

1. If you are using frozen juice, let it sit out and warm up

2. Open the can, add the grape juice to a pitcher and water

36

3. Pour the lemonade into a glass

4. Mix the lemonade and grape juice together in a glass or in the pitcher

5. Drink up

aunt libba's fancy sherbet

Try not to touch your face and hair after your hands are clean

INGREDIENTS

1 scoop of lime sherbet
1 cup of thawed frozen strawberries

1. Put a nice scoop of lime sherbet in a bowl

2. Top with the thawed, frozen strawberries

3. Eat with a big spoon

Naughty baRs

INGREDIENTS

2 tablespoons of peanut butter
1/3 cup of cereal that is high in vitamins
2 tablespoons of chocolate chips
1 tablespoon of honey
1 tablespoon of powdered milk
(optional)

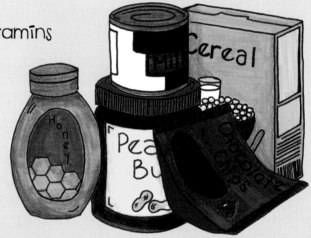

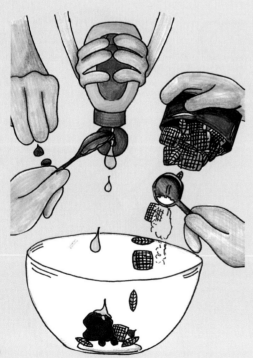

1. Put all of your ingredients into a bowl and mix with your hands

2. Make a ball the size of your fist with the ingredients

3. Shape your peanut butter ball mixture into a bar

4. Put your naughty bar into the refrigerator

5. Wash your hands

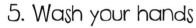

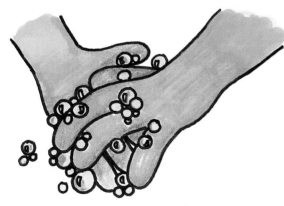

6. When your naughty bar gets hard, eat it up!

41

CHOColatE aNd vaNilla SwiRl

INGREDIENTS

1 cup of low fat vanilla yogurt
Cinnamon
Chocolate syrup
Low-fat graham crackers
Sliced apples and peaches
and whole strawberries

1. Put low-fat vanilla yogurt into a small bowl

42

3. Put a little chocolate syrup in the yogurt

Chocolate Syrup

2. Sprinkle some cinnamon on the yogurt

4. Mix up the yogurt, cinnamon and chocolate syrup

5. Dip the graham crackers and fruit into the yogurt and eat up!

43

tiME out paRfait

INGREDIENTS

Vanilla low-fat yogurt
Your favorite fruit (cut up)
Brain food (page 16)

1. Put yogurt in the
bottom of a small glass

3. Put more yogurt on top of the fruit

2. Make a layer of your favorite fruit

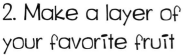

4. Make a layer of trail mix on top of the yogurt

5. Get a spoon and dig in!

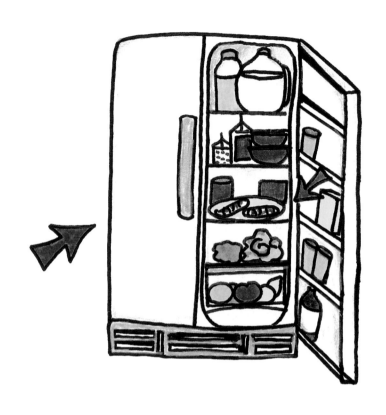

always put youR food away
WHEN you aRE fiNishEd

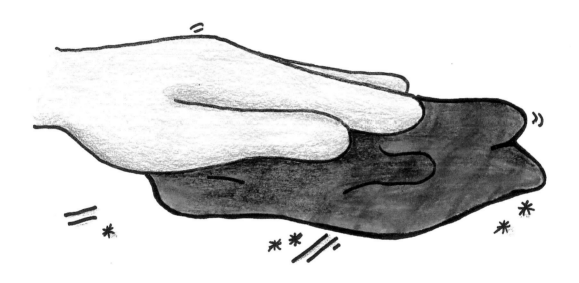

KEEp youR Food SuRFacE clEaN

Measurements

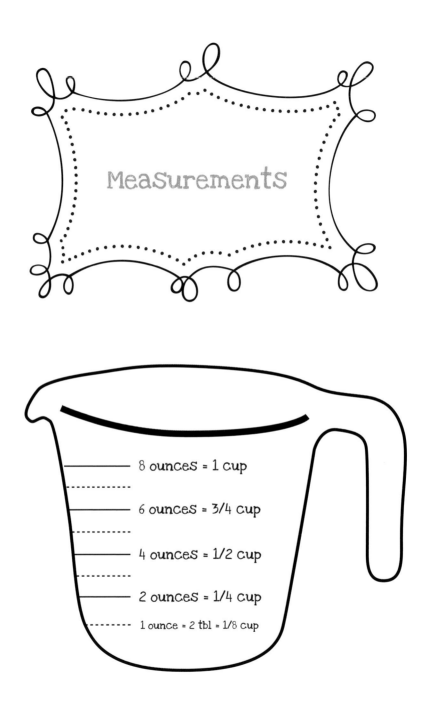

8 ounces = 1 cup

6 ounces = 3/4 cup

4 ounces = 1/2 cup

2 ounces = 1/4 cup

1 ounce = 2 tbl = 1/8 cup

Notes and
Favorite Recipes

_____

_____

_____

_____

_____

_____

Notes and
Favorite Recipes

_____

_____

_____

_____

_____

_____

Notes and
Favorite Recipes

_____

_____

_____

_____

_____

_____

Notes and
Favorite Recipes

_____

_____

_____

_____

_____

_____